심우철
복습종이

합격영어 1. 구문

심우철 지음

기본서 N회독 복습종이

모든 문장이 쉽게 해석되는 구문 독해 법칙 전수

문장 구조 이해를 통한 빠른 해석 능력 배양

커넥츠 공단기
인터넷 강의
gong.conects.com

Contents

목차

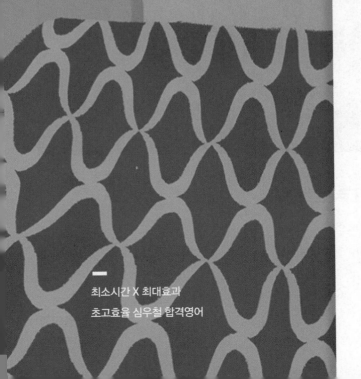

최소시간 X 최대효과
초고효율 심우철 합격영어

❖ 다음 밑줄 친 부분의 품사를 쓰세요.

> 예제 He bought a digital camera.
> 품사 대명사 / 동사 / 관사 / 형용사 / 명사

01 My brother is really smart.

품사

02 She can speak various languages.

품사

03 I must finish my homework today.

품사

04 My house is right behind my school.

품사

05 There are many customers in the store.

품사

06 The man planted a tree in the garden.

품사

07 I did not sleep well for three days.

품사

08 She told me about the accident yesterday.

품사

09 He always washes his hands before every meal.

품사

10 The expert is in full agreement with our policy.

품사

11 These chemical changes occur so naturally.

품사

❶ 다음이 무슨 구인지 쓰세요.

01   the wavelength or color of the emitted light (2022, 국가직 9급)

01
wavelength 파장
emit 방출하다

02   one of the most common mistakes in reasoning (2015, 지방직 7급)

02
reasoning 추론

03   about the advantage of language practice

04   an empirical analysis of over 400 articles

04
empirical 실증적인, 경험에 의거한
analysis 분석

05   over two million acres of land in the country

05
country 시골, 전원

06   additional emphasis on the virtue of modesty

06
emphasis 강조
virtue 미덕, 덕목
modesty 겸손

07 a simple way of easing the stress of driving (2020, 국가직 9급)

07
ease 완화하다

08 the excitement of leaving for a foreign country

09 the availability of oxygen in many parts of the sea (2021, 국가직 9급)

09
availability 이용 가능성

10 one of the most destructive forms of all the storms

10
destructive 파괴적인

11 years of research / lots of students / a kind of sports

12 tens of students from several colleges around Dublin

13 the earliest and most effective machines available to humans

(2019, 국가직 9급)

14 realistic animated scenes of fish and other underwater objects

(2022, 국가직 9급)

15 lots of people at the clubs, pubs, and bars in downtown

16 a record of denying proper medical care to prisoners (2019, 서울시 9급)

17 some of the resource materials ready for promotion of movies

18 the religious, philosophical, moral, and political values of a culture

(2019, 국가직 9급)

19 the unchallenged leader in transportation for a hundred years

20 one of the most famous yet mysterious celebrities of recent times

20
celebrity 유명인사
recent 최근의

21 with his ability to fuse serious content with humorous style

(2019, 국가직 9급)

21
fuse 융합시키다
content 내용

22 15 years of research on U.S. employment and the minimum wage

22
minimum wage 최저 임금

23 the poor performance of American students on various international tests

23
performance (수행의) 성과, 성적
various 다양한

24 his absolutely outstanding performance in an exceptionally difficult condition

24
exceptionally 유난히

25 three rows of benches on each side of the stage and six rows in front of the principal

25
row 줄
principal 교장

26 I bought <u>a very expensive car</u>.

I bought <u>a very expensive car from the car-dealer's shop 5 years ago</u>.

I bought <u>a very expensive car with leather seats, a comfortable house, and costly gems</u>.

27 the process of sensing our environment through touch, taste, sight, sound, and smell (2014, 사회복지직 9급)

28 the inability to consistently sleep well for a period of less than a month (2018, 국가직 9급)

29 one of the fundamental rights of every human being without distinction of race

30 the size of the nerves connecting the eyes and the ears to the centers of the brain (2017, 국가직 9급)

31 the development of new types of products and services and new forms and methods of distribution

31
distribution 분배, 유통

32 the connection between acting on the feedback and negative sanctions such as being laid off or fired (2019, 국가직 9급)

32
sanction 제재
lay off (구조조정 등의 이유로)
해고하다
fire (업무능력 등의 이유로)
해고하다

33 a one-for-one relationship between income of the bottom fifth of the population and per capita GDP (2017, 국가직 9급)

33
per capita GDP 1인당 국내 총생산

34 the growing need for information and communication technologies to fight climate change and to build greener, more environmentally friendly economies

34
need 필요성
climate 기후

⓫ 다음 문장을 해석하세요.

01 Lamela is the author of over 250 articles.

02 The price of gold goes up along with unemployment.

03 Minor is the legal description of a person under the age of 18.

04 The passenger angry about the delay of the flight asked for a refund.

05 Learning is a hope to the poor, an honor to the rich, and a comfort to the aged.

06 Exports declined in 1965 and 1966, both in terms of quantity and total shipments.

07 The children full of hope for the future own a positive point of view about things.

08 Individual human being cannot exist, without the cooperation of others in society.

09 Basketball legend Michael Jordan practiced shooting for about 10,000 times in a day.

10 In spite of a few clashes, the relationship between the police and protesters was peaceful.

11 Online advertising is basically a one-way communication similar to network television.

12 The e-book applications available on tablet computers employ touchscreen technology. (2020, 지방직 9급)

12
employ 이용하다, 쓰다

13 Hundreds of statues of Greek gods such as Apollo, Jupiter, and Neptune stood in the gardens. (2020, 지방직 9급)

13
statue 조각상

14 The reason for the ubiquitous production of light by the microorganisms of the sea remains obscure. (2010, 국회직 8급)

14
ubiquitous 어디에나 있는
microorganism 미생물
obscure 불분명한, 애매한

15 About 83 percent of the cost of the health service comes from general taxation.

15
health service 건강 보험
general 일반적인
taxation 조세

16 The rates of gun homicide and other gun crimes in the United States have dropped since highs in the early 1990's. (2020, 국가직 9급)

16
gun homicide 총기 살인

17 Reducing water pollution and cleaning and restoring polluted water to its natural state can help to stretch our supply of fresh water.

17
reduce 줄이다
pollution 오염
restore 회복시키다
stretch 늘리다

18 The phenomenal achievements of African-Americans have drawn little attention in U.S. despite their great significance.

18
phenomenal 경이적인
despite ~에도 불구하고
significance 중요성

19 A sudden increase of population over the carrying capacity of the land causes a deterioration in the standard of living and enlarges the total of the malnourished.

19
capacity 수용량, 용량, 능력
deterioration 악화, 저하
standard 수준, 표준
enlarge 크게 하다, 확대하다
malnourished 영양실조의

20 After its launch in 2010, Instagram became one of the top social media networks, with one million registered users in two months.

20
registered 등록된

21 In June 2016, as presidential candidate, Donald Trump launched a trade war against Chinese economic practices, as a reaction against a leadership class worshipping globalism.

21
launch 시작하다, 나서다
practice 관행
worship 숭배하다

Chapter 03 **문장의 5형식**

UNIT 2. 문장의 형식

❖ 다음을 해석하세요.

01 Women with a history of depression seem more vulnerable to stroke.

> **01**
> depression 우울증
> vulnerable 취약한
> stroke 뇌졸중

02 Warm ocean water moving underneath the vast glaciers is causing them to melt even more quickly. (2022. 국가직 9급)

> **02**
> underneath ~의 아래에
> glacier 빙하
> melt 녹다

03 In 1976, at just 21, Jobs and Wozniak started Apple Computer in the Jobs' family garage.

04 Modern medicine has seen human race rely less on manual efforts and more on technology.

> **04**
> manual 수동의, 손으로 하는

05 The number of people with diabetes rose from 108 million in 1980 to 422 million in 2014.

> **05**
> diabetes 당뇨병

06 In 1857, Alfred Russel Wallace sent Darwin a paper regarding the evolution of species. (2013, 국회직 8급)

06
regarding ~에 관한

07 Bruce Lipstadt had the left hemisphere of his brain removed when he was five and a half years old. (2013, 국회직 9급)

07
hemisphere 반구
remove 제거하다

08 A vacation policy allowing employees to take unlimited time off sounds unreasonable for any company.

08
unlimited 무제한의
unreasonable 불합리한, 부당한

09 Gun violence in the United States results in tens of thousands of deaths and injuries annually.

09
violence 폭력
annually 매년

10 Advances in the development of electric cars will help us to be less dependent on oil for transportation.

10
advance 진보, 발전

11 She heard her father going down the stairs to the garden and slowly raised her head to look out the window.

12 Coffee with bitter and slightly acidic flavor has a stimulating effect in humans, primarily due to its caffeine content.

12
acidic 산성의
stimulate 자극하다

13 Like many smartphone owners, he gave himself too much time in staring at the glowing black rectangle in his pocket.

13
glow 빛나다
rectangle 직사각형

14 Many people consider her the most influential social science researcher of the twentieth century.

14
consider 간주하다, 생각하다
influential 영향력 있는
social science 사회과학

15 The thin and flexible bags made up of impenetrable material keep the food unaffected by environmental factors.

15
flexible 신축성 있는
impenetrable 뚫을 수 없는
unaffected 영향을 받지 않은

16 The accident in 1986 at Chernobyl reminded the world that we should use nuclear power responsibly.

16
nuclear power 원자력
responsibly 책임감 있게

17 All possible combinations and concentrations of different elements in the same resource made the process even more efficient.

17
combination 조합, 결합
concentration 집중, 농축

18 Vitamins, unlike carbohydrates, fats, and proteins, do not produce energy in our bodies but they regulate many of the body's functions.

18
carbohydrate 탄수화물
regulate 조절하다

19 All airlines in Brazil currently permit all passengers to check-in two pieces of baggage on international flights to and from the country.

19
currently 현재

20 Coca-Cola invented in the late 19th century by John Stith Pemberton is a leading supplier of the world soft-drink market throughout the 20th century.

20
leading 선도하는

21 The uncertain economic condition of recent years has caused union and management representatives to explore many ways of handling labor problems.

21
uncertain 불확실한
economic 경제의
union (노동)조합
representative 대표
handle 다루다

22 Some companies offer all students online teaching alternatives instead of classroom teaching due to the risk of infection of the coronavirus.

22
infection 감염

23 According to Dr. Greenspan, Bertrand Russell joined the heated intellectual debate about the selection of the best political governance structure for China.

23
heated 열띤
debate 논쟁, 토론

24 Nevertheless, travelling gives travelers a couple of advantages, such as making them explore the unknown and experience new cultures different from theirs. (2013, 기상직 9급)

24
advantage 이점

25 After a progressive program to teach the kids to wash their hands properly several times during the day, diarrhea cases dropped 69% and influenza cases dropped 55%.

25
progressive 전진하는, 점진적인
diarrhea 설사
case 사례
influenza 독감

26 Because of the impact on the environment with regards to the clearing of land for coffee-growing and water use, the markets for fair trade and organic coffee grow, notably in the USA.

26
clearing 개척
notably 특히

27 According to the Korea Statistics' data on the average annual income of an urban household with two or more people, buying a median-priced home in Seoul requires 9.2 years.

27
income 소득, 수입

UNIT 3. 그 밖의 문장의 형식

❖ 다음을 해석하세요.

01 The reflective mood of the song reminded him of a recent trip to the Himalayas.

01
reflective 사색적인, 반영하는

02 A carefully expressed purpose will help anchor your essay and keep it from aimlessly floating all over. (2012, 법원직 9급)

02
anchor 고정시키다
aimlessly 목적 없이
float 떠다니다

03 A business enterprise should look upon consumers' demands as the most important thing.

03
enterprise 기업

04 The Korean government presented coach Guus Hiddink with honorary citizenship and a passport.

04
present 수여하다
honorary 명예의
citizenship 시민권
passport 여권

05 A number of gun advocates consider ownership a birthright and an essential part of the nation's heritage. (2020, 국가직 9급)

05
advocate 옹호자, 지지자
birthright 생득권
heritage 유산

06 Across the nation, people from all walks of life took measures to keep the flu from spreading among their workforce.

07 In an effort to curb my distracting explanation, the proctor led me to an empty seat and put a test booklet in front of me. (2018, 지방직 9급)

08 Also, a very rapid response time may deprive the parties concerned of the opportunity to solve the problems by themselves.

09 For example, in American culture, it is easy to think of work simply as a means to accumulate money and make a living.

10 The pandemic coronavirus has suspended production of the movies and stripped film industry workers of their jobs.

11 Ignorance and superstition about law and legal process prevent some members from benefiting from modern civil system of justice.

12 The disharmony between congress and the president during economic slowdown robbed them of some prestige and confused people looking for stability.

13 Many psychologists see the home as the most natural learning environment, and originally the home was the classroom, long before schools were established. (2020, 국가직 9급)

14 The receptionist on the second floor will provide you with information concerning benefits available to you in connection with the termination of your employment.

15 The apparent failure of the U.S. intelligence on Iraq reminds us of the need for a thorough review of all information that has so far surfaced concerning the North Korean WMD.

* WMD(Weapons of Mass Destruction) 대량 살상 무기

16 Andrew Carnegie, as one of the richest people in history, led the remainder of his life to large-scale philanthropy, with special emphasis on local libraries, world peace, education, and scientific research.

UNIT 4. 품사편 총정리

❖ 다음을 해석하세요.

01 Russia and Saudi Arabia helped drive oil prices to their lowest levels in 18 years.

02 Because society has deprived women of many equal rights, feminists have fought for equality. (2014, 경찰직 1차)

03 Last year, more than half of the box-office revenues of Japan's movie industry came from animations.

03
box-office 흥행의, 인기를 끄는
revenue 수익

04 Many people in South Korean society consider education as the main propeller of social mobility for themselves.

04
propeller 추진기
social mobility 사회적 유동[이동]성

05 If you want to have one of the most enjoyable and personally profitable evenings of your life, don't pass up this course.

05
enjoyable 즐거운
profitable 유익한
pass up 놓치다

06 Spiders live in all different kinds of climates and environments from blazing deserts to damp caves and towering mountain tops.

(2009, 국가직 7급)

06
blazing 타오르는
damp 축축한
towering 우뚝 솟은

07 Governments should continuously remind themselves that a mix of short-term relief and medium-term recovery efforts can stop droughts from turning into famines.

07
recovery 복구, 회복
famine 기근

08 English midwives would place a loaf of bread at the foot of a new mother's bed to prevent the woman and her child from being kidnapped by evil spirits. (2015, 국가직 7급)

08
midwife 산파
loaf 덩어리
kidnap 납치하다

09 However, elevated levels and/or long term exposure to air pollution can lead to more serious symptoms and conditions affecting human health. (2016, 법원직 9급)

09
elevated 높은, 고상한
lead to 초래하다
symptom 증상
condition 상태
affect 영향을 주다

10 An increased awareness of the effects of plastic bags has caused many states and countries to implement plastic bag related legislation. (2018, 경찰직 2차)

10
awareness 인식
implement 시행하다
legislation 법률의 제정

11 Globalization refers to increasing global connectivity, integration and interdependence in the economic, social, technological, cultural, political, and ecological spheres. (2008, 지방직 7급)

11
globalization 세계화
refer to ~를 나타내다; ~에 대해 언급하다
connectivity 연결성
integration 통합
interdependence 상호의존
ecological 생태계의, 생태학의
sphere 분야

12 Doctors think of cosmetic surgery as an improvement on normal parts of the body with the only purpose of improving a person's appearance or removing signs of aging.

12
cosmetic surgery 성형수술
appearance 외모

13 Workers in manufacturing jobs are likely to suffer serious health problems as a result of the noise, or the stress from mechanical requirements of the assembly line.

13
be likely to ~하기 쉽다
suffer 겪다
requirement 요구
assembly line 조립라인

14 The viability of reclaimed water for indirect potable reuse should be assessed with regard to quantity and reliability of raw water supplies, the quality of reclaimed water, and cost effectiveness.

14
viability 실행 가능성
reclaimed 재생된
potable 마시기에 적합한
assess 평가하다
with regard to ~에 관해서
reliability 신뢰도
raw 익히지 않은, 날것의

15 Millions of people suffering from watery and stinging eyes, pounding headaches, sinus issues, and itchy throats, sought refuge from the debilitating air by scouring stores for air filters and face masks. (2017, 서울시 9급)

15
watery 눈물이 흐르는
stinging 따가운
pounding 지끈거리는
sinus 부비강
itchy 가려운
debilitating 쇠약하게 하는
scour 샅샅이 뒤지다

16 Since industry and commerce are the largest users of electrical energy, using less electricity would mean a reduced industrial capacity and fewer jobs in the affected industries and therefore an unfavorable change in our economic structure.

16
electrical 전기의
reduce 줄이다
capacity 능력
affected 영향을 받은
unfavorable 좋지 않은

17 Persons with great potential ability sometimes fall down on the job because of laziness or lack of interest in the job, while persons with mediocre talents have often achieved excellent results through their industry and their loyalty to the interests of their employers.

17
potential 잠재적인
fall down on the job 일을 제대로 하지 않다
laziness 게으름, 나태함
mediocre 보통의, 이류의
industry 근면성
loyalty 충실, 충성

18 As a principal dictionary of the English language, the Oxford English Dictionary provides scholars and academic researchers with a comprehensive resource, in addition to describing usage in its many variations throughout the world.

18
principal 주요한
scholar 학자
comprehensive 포괄적인, 종합적인
in addition to ~일 뿐 아니라
variation 변형

UNIT 2. 관계사·의문사 해석법

❖ 다음을 해석하세요.

01 From time to time we must look up words whose meanings we do not know.

01
from time to time 때때로
look up 찾아보다

02 There are many organizations whose sole purpose is to help mentally retarded children.

02
organization 기관, 단체
sole 유일한
retarded 정신 발달이 늦은

03 One of Heungseon Daewongun's major achievements was rebuilding Gyeongbok Palace which was burnt down during the Japanese invasion in 1592.

03
rebuild 재건하다
palace 궁전
invasion 침략

04 Environmental scientists chose two Chicago public housing projects, both of which had some buildings with lots of trees nearby, and some with practically none.

04
public housing (저소득층) 공공 주택
practically 사실상

05 Similarly, corn in Latin America is traditionally ground or soaked with limestone, which makes available a B vitamin in the corn, the absence of which would otherwise lead to a deficiency disease.

05
similarly 마찬가지로
grind 갈다
soak 담그다
limestone 석회암
available 이용할 수 있는
absence 부재
otherwise 그렇지 않으면
deficiency disease 결핍성 질환

06 There are times when even the best leaders lose their emotional balance. (2020, 경찰직 1차)

06
emotional 정서적인, 감정적인

07 Clearly, modern societies are facing a major change into a new economic system where human resourcefulness counts far more than natural resources.

07
face 직면하다
economic 경제의
human resourcefulness 인적 자원
count 중요하다
natural resource 천연자원

08 Climate change has narrowed the range where bumblebees are found in North America and Europe in recent decades, according to a recent study, published in the journal *Science*. (2017, 사회복지직 9급)

08
narrow 좁히다
bumblebee 호박벌

09 I approached the tree in which many soldiers had been hanged in the war.

09
approach 접근하다, 다가가다
hang 교수형에 처하다

10 The origin of new species, which the nineteenth-century English naturalist Charles Darwin once referred to as "the mystery of mysteries," is the natural process of speciation responsible for generating this remarkable diversity of living creatures with whom humans share the planet. (2020, 국가직 9급)

10
naturalist 자연주의자
speciation 종 분화
remarkable 놀라운, 주목할 만한

11 Have you decided which one you're going to buy?

12 Who we are is reflected in what we won't eat, as well as what we will. (2013, 법원직 9급)

12
reflect 반영하다

13 Nobody could understand where we ever got money enough to keep us with food in our bellies. (2021, 법원직 9급)

13
belly 배

14 One of the classic answers to this question is that politics is about who gets what, when and how. (2020, 국회직 8급)

14
classic 전형적인, 고전적인

15 I am convinced that there is a direct correlation between job satisfaction and how empowered people are to fully execute their job without someone shadowing them every step of the way. (2021, 지방직 9급)

15
correlation 상관관계
empower 권한을 주다
execute 수행하다
shadow 따라다니다

16 A model producing a weather forecast will give a prediction for what the conditions will be like in different parts of the world just a few days into the future. (2017, 기상직 9급)

16
prediction 예측
condition 상황

17 Not knowing what to do, I climbed up to the top of a tall tree, from which I looked around to see if I could discover anything that could give me hope.

17
look around 둘러보다

18 Leaders who carefully choose which seminars and conferences to attend may help themselves strengthen their contribution to their personal developmental goals. (2016, 지방직 9급)

18
attend 참석하다
strengthen 강화하다
contribution 기여

19 We begin to philosophize when we try to decide which pleasures are most important to us, for example, looking slim and trim on the one hand or enjoying satisfying meals on the other.

19
philosophize 철학적으로 사색하다
trim 잘 가꾼, 깔끔한
satisfying 만족스러운

20 You have either more money or more time, whichever you need most. (2015, 지방직 9급)

21 Whenever you catch yourself having a fit of worry, stop and change your thoughts. (2018, 국가직 9급)

21
fit (감정의) 북받침, 격발; (병의) 발작

22 Those who learn English as a foreign language tend to read English texts slowly and consult a dictionary whenever they come across unfamiliar words. (2015, 지방직 7급)

22
consult 찾아보다, 참고하다
come across 마주치다, 우연히 발견하다
unfamiliar 낯선

23 He was thought of as the most flattering man in our company since he accepted whatever his superiors suggested without reflective thinking. (2017, 국회직 9급)

23
flattering 아첨하는
accept 받아들이다
superior 상사
reflective 반성적인

24 Your GPS receiver can tell you your exact location and give you directions to wherever you need to go, no matter where you are on the planet! (2018, 법원직 9급)

24
exact 정확한
direction 방향

25 Whatever the source of the images in our sleeping brains may be, we need to be cautious about interpreting our own dreams or anyone else's.

25
cautious 조심하는
interpret 해석하다

26 No matter how upset you are, keep the feedback job-related and never criticize someone personally because of an inappropriate action. (2014, 국가직 9급)

26
inappropriate 부적절한

27 But the public also has a great interest in science, as is shown by the large audiences for science fiction. (2019, 서울시 7급)

28 As might be expected, older workers stay at the same job for a longer period than younger ones do. (2017, 교육행정직 9급)

29 Those who have doubts about their uses are worried that surveillance cameras are not as effective in preventing crime as have been believed. (2015, 경찰직 1차)

29
doubt 의구심
surveillance 감시
effective 효과적인

UNIT 3. 절 해석법

① ⋯⋯ 문장 중간에 that이 나오면...

❖ 다음을 해석하세요.

01 His hiring concluded an exhaustive process that collected input from all segments of the university. (2014, 지방직 9급)

01
hiring 채용
exhaustive 철저한
input 조언, 의견
segment 부분

02 The modernization theory of aging suggests that the role and status of older adults are inversely related to technological progress. (2019, 법원직 9급)

02
aging 고령화
inversely 반비례적으로

03 Researchers have developed a new model that they said will provide better estimates about the North Atlantic right whale population. (2017, 국가직 9급)

03
estimates 추정치
population 개체 수

04 When the moderator asked him if age was a concern in the election, he famously replied that he would not make age an issue of that campaign. (2015, 교육행정직 9급)

04
moderator 사회자
concern 우려, 걱정
election 선거
campaign 운동

05 People in his experiments were told that a spot of light projected on the wall would move and were instructed to estimate the amount of movement. (2015, 지방직 9급)

05
spot 지점
project 투영하다
instruct 지시하다
estimate 추정하다

06 From a mother's embracing of her baby that forms the foundation of the self, to the holding of hands between a son and his dying father that allows a final letting go, touch is our most intimate and powerful form of communication.

06
embrace 포옹하다, 받아들이다
foundation 기본, 기초, 토대
self 자아
dying 죽어 가는
intimate 친근한

07 Chile is a Latin American country that throughout most of the twentieth century was marked by a relatively advanced liberal democracy on the one hand and only moderate economic growth, which forced it to become a food importer, on the other. (2011, 지방직 9급)

07
liberal 자유주의의
democracy 민주주의
moderate 보통의
importer 수입국

참고 예외적인 경우

01 He informed her that his baby had a special disease.

01
disease 질병

02 His idea is that people should try to preserve our environment.

02
preserve 보존하다
environment 환경

03 The three-penny tax on tea was so exorbitant that our revolutionary fathers fought and died. (2013, 서울시 7급)

03
exorbitant 과도한, 지나친
revolutionary 혁명의, 혁명적인

04 I agree to the idea that good behavior must be reinforced with incentives.

04
reinforce 강화하다
incentive 인센티브, 장려책

② ⸺ 문장 중간에 「주어(S) + 동사(V)」가 나오면...

❖ 다음을 해석하세요.

01 The short-term chaos we see with weather forecasts tends to smooth out over decades and centuries. (2017, 기상직 9급)

01
chaos 혼돈
smooth 잠잠해지다

02 When you concentrate on the one task of your priorities, you will find you have energy that you didn't even know you had. (2018, 지방직 9급)

02
concentrate 집중하다
priority 우선사항

03 A lot of our fear of death is about losing the things we have built up, but elderly people let go of their attachment to these things.

(2017, 서울시 7급)

03
let go (of) ~에서 손을 놓다, 풀어 주다; 해고하다
attachment 애착

04 When Jesse and Rachel got married, they knew they wanted to live in a traditional nuclear family — mother, father, and biological children. (2008, 국가직 9급)

04
traditional 전통적인
nuclear family 핵가족
biological child 친자

05 A nearly equal number of people also said they would seek emergency medical care for their pets before obtaining it for themselves. (2015, 법원직 9급)

05
equal 같은
seek 구하다
obtain 받다

06 The study showed the ability of students to retain knowledge about words improved after one night sleep even if the students lost some of that knowledge during the day.

06
retain 유지하다; 보유하다

07 The Native Americans they met were considered to be savage peoples, with none of the characteristics of European civilization, nor did they possess true religion according to this view. (2015, 교육행정직 9급)

07
savage 야만적인
civilization 문명
possess 지니다
religion 종교

08 Dr. Weil suggests this antioxidant protects our heart by lowering cholesterol and boosting metabolism, and guards against cancer by removing radicals that can damage cells and push them in the direction of uncontrolled growth. (2014, 사회복지직 9급)

08
antioxidant 항산화제
boost 촉진시키다
metabolism 신진대사
guard against ~이 생기지 않도록
조심하다
radical 라디칼, 근치 (질환의 근본이
되는 구역 부근)

09 Advertising studies in Martin Lindstorm's book Brand Sense suggest that although most contemporary commercial messages are aimed at our eyes, many of the emotional moments people remember on a given day are actually prompted by smell. (2014, 법원직 9급)

09
contemporary 현대의
commercial 상업의
aim 겨냥하다
emotional 감정적인
prompt 유발하다

③ ⸺문장 맨 앞에 「명사 + 관계대명사(관계부사)」가 나오면...

❖ 다음을 해석하세요.

01 The task which confronts him is not different from that which faced his predecessor. (2008, 국가직 7급)

01
confront 직면하다
different from ~와 다른
face 직면하다
predecessor 전임자

02 The President, who is elected by nationwide direct ballot, is the head of state and serves a single five-year term. (2018, 국회직 8급)

02
nationwide 전국적인
ballot 투표, 선거
serve 근무하다, 임기 동안 일하다

03 Professor Taylor, who wrote "What are Children for?," believes that the status of fatherhood has been affected by modern life. (2012, 국가직 9급)

03
status 지위
fatherhood 아버지
modern 현대의

04 The major reason why spelling in English is difficult is that modern English spelling shows old English pronunciation. (2011, 지방직 9급)

04
pronunciation 발음

05 A man who shoplifted from the Woolworth's store in Shanton in 1952 recently sent the shop an anonymous letter of apology.
(2012, 국가직 9급)

05
shoplift 가게 물건을 훔치다
anonymous 익명인
apology 사과

06 Thus a person with a high metabolic rate who consumes greater calories may actually be producing more harmful forms of oxygen than someone with a slower metabolic rate. (2020, 경찰직 1차)

06
metabolic rate 신진대사율

07 One study that measured participants' exposure to thirty-seven major negative events found a curvilinear relationship between lifetime adversity and mental health. (2020, 경찰직 1차)

07
participant 참가자
exposure 노출
curvilinear 곡선적인
adversity 역경, 고난

08 The right to wield power and the extent to which an authority should wield power must be questioned and negotiated lest the power be abusive and lead to injustice and unfairness. (2015, 지방직 9급)

08
wield 행사하다
authority 권한, (보통 pl.) 권위자, 정부 당국
negotiate 협상하다
lest ~하지 않도록
abusive 남용하는

09 One of the challenges we face in the world today is that a lot of the information we get about other people and places comes from the advertising and entertainment we see in the media. (2014, 국가직 9급)

09
challenge 도전
face 직면하다

10 A Caucasian territory whose inhabitants have resisted Russian rule almost since its beginnings in the late 18th century has been the center of the incessant political turmoil. (2013, 지방직 9급)

10
territory 영토
inhabitant 주민
resist 저항하다
beginning 초기
incessant 끊임없는
turmoil 혼란

UNIT 4. 기타 접속사 해석

❖ 다음을 해석하세요.

01 The sun is slowly getting brighter as its core contracts and heats up.

(2020, 경찰직 1차)

01
core (사물의) 중심부
contract 수축하다, 줄어들다; 계약하다; (병에) 걸리다
heat up 뜨거워지다, 가열되다

02 Sarah frequently hurts others when she criticizes their work because she is so outspoken. (2010, 국가직 9급)

02
frequently 자주
hurt 다치게 하다
criticize 비판하다
outspoken 노골적으로 말하는

03 Remember to go through the pockets before you put those trousers in the washing machine. (2015, 경찰직 1차)

03
go through 살펴보다
washing machine 세탁기

04 Although the actress experienced much turmoil in her career, she never disclosed to anyone that she was unhappy. (2019, 국가직 9급)

04
turmoil 혼란, 소란
disclose 드러내다, 밝히다

05 Similarly, if pain existed but fear did not, a child would burn himself again and again, because fear would not warn him to keep away from the fire that had burnt him before. (2017, 지방직 9급)

05
exist 존재하다
fear 두려움
burn 태우다, 타다
warn 경고하다
keep away from ~을 멀리하다

06 That is, if you can convince yourself that the first draft isn't your best writing and can be made more effective with additional thought and some revision, then it will be easier to get started.

06
that is 즉, 다시 말해
convince 납득시키다
draft 초고
revision 수정

07 While I cannot promise you that your temporary contract will be extended every time it comes up for review, I can tell you that there do not seem to be any obstacles to further extensions.

07
temporary 일시적인
contract 계약
extend 연장하다
obstacle 장애물
extension 연장

08 Normally, these metals and chemicals may not cause many problems, because as they are taken in by the body, it works to get rid of them. (2017, 소방직 9급 하반기)

08
chemical 화학 물질
take in ~을 흡수하다; 속이다
get rid of 제거하다

09 There are growing concerns that, as the fourth industrial revolution deepens our individual and collective relationships with technology, it may negatively affect our social skills and ability to empathize. (2017, 기상직 9급)

09
concern 걱정, 우려
industrial revolution 산업혁명
deepen 심화시키다
collective 집단의
negatively 부정적으로
empathize 공감하다

10 Despite the fact that the priority should be to create infrastructure such as roads, schools, and hospitals, what often happens is that incompetent and corrupt officials end up misusing or stealing the money. (2018, 지방직 7급)

10
priority 우선사항
infrastructure 기반시설
incompetent 무능한
corrupt 부패한
misuse 남용하다

11 In his book *Feminine Faces*, Clovis Chappel wrote that when the Roman city of Pompeii was being excavated, the body of a woman was found mummified by the volcanic ashes of Mount Vesuvius.

excavate 발굴하다
mummify 미라로 만들다
volcanic 화산의
ash 재

12 In particular they discovered that when language learners attempt to understand speech in another language, it activates and energizes the brainstem — as ancient part of the brain. (2014, 법원직 9급)

12
in particular 특히
attempt 시도하다
activate 활성화시키다
energize 활기를 북돋우다
ancient 오래된

13 Because I mainly study traditional Chinese music, it's interesting to compare traditional Korean music with traditional Chinese music, because there are some elements that have actually remained with traditional Korean music that are no longer found in the traditional Chinese music. (2017, 경찰직 1차)

13
traditional 전통의
compare 비교하다
remain 남다

UNIT 2. 분사구문

❖ 다음을 해석하세요.

01 Putting a man to death by hanging or electric shock is an extremely cruel form of punishment.

01
cruel 잔인한
punishment 형벌, 처벌

02 Asking a working writer what he thinks about critics is like asking a lamppost how it feels about dogs.

02
lamppost 가로등, 가로등 기둥

03 Hearing what other people have to say, especially about concepts we regard as foundational, is like opening a window in our minds and in our hearts. (2020, 국가직 9급)

03
foundational 기본의, 기초적인

04 To bring about an increase in exports, it is important for us to sell commodities of excellent quality and a low price. (2014, 국회직 8급)

04
bring about 초래하다, 가져오다
export 수출
commodity 상품

05 Unable to finish college because of a lack of money, he took a job as a playground instructor earning thirty dollars a week.

05
instructor 코치, 강사

06 To navigate in the dark, a microbat flies with its mouth open, emitting high-pitched squeaks that humans cannot hear. (2019, 서울시 9급)

06
emit (소리 등을) 내다
squeak 끽하는 소리

07 A new manner to represent the problem is suddenly discovered, leading to a different path to a solution heretofore unpredicted. (2020, 경찰직 1차)

07
represent 표현하다, 나타내다
discover 발견하다
lead to ~로 이어지다
heretofore 이전에는, 지금까지는

08 Therefore, the value of the art results not only from its uniqueness but from its being the source from which reproductions are made.

08
uniqueness 독특함, 유일함
reproduction 복제, 재현, 복제품

09 To prevent software from being copied illegally and protect the copyright, above all, software companies should lower the price of their goods to a reasonable price.

09
illegally 불법적으로
copyright 저작권
reasonable 합리적인

10 When giving performance feedback, you should consider the recipient's past performance and your estimate of his or her future potential in designing its frequency, amount, and content. (2019, 국가직 9급)

10
recipient 받는 사람
estimate 추정
potential 잠재력
design 설계하다, 의도하다
content 내용

11 In 2013, a state of emergency in Beijing resulting from the dangerously high levels of pollution led to chaos in the transportation system, forcing airlines to cancel flights due to low visibility. (2017, 서울시 9급)

11
result from ~에서 기인하다
pollution 오염
chaos 혼란
transportation 교통
visibility 가시성

12 It has also been hypothesized that the emission of light on disturbance is advantageous to the plankton in making the predators of the plankton conspicuous to their predators.

12
hypothesize 가정하다
emission 발산
disturbance 방해
predator 포식자
conspicuous 눈에 띄는

13 Understanding the movements of heavenly bodies and the relationship between angles and distances, medieval travelers were able to create a system of longitude and latitude.

13
heavenly body 천체
medieval 중세의
longitude 경도
latitude 위도

14 To escape the chore of scraping with an old credit card, many people use warm water only to find their windscreen freezing over again once they are on the road, with potentially critical consequences.

15 These giant cacti have great value in landscape gardening, and poachers can earn thousands of dollars by uprooting them and selling them to nurseries. (2017, 국회직 8급)

16 Medical illnesses such as stroke, a heart attack, cancer, Parkinson's disease, and hormonal disorders can cause depressive illness, making the sick person apathetic and unwilling to care for his or her physical needs, thus prolonging the recovery period.

UNIT 3. 준동사 해석법

① ······ 문장 맨 앞에 RVing나 p.p.가 나오면...

❖ 다음을 해석하세요.

01 Protecting the health and safety of everyone in the facility should be the first priority. (2018, 서울시 7급)

01
facility 시설, 기관

02 Recognizing the healing power of humor, many hospitals are starting to take laughing matters seriously.

02
recognize 인정하다
matter 문제

03 Monocropping vast fields with the same genetically uniform seeds helps boost yield and meet immediate hunger needs. (2017, 소방직 9급)

03
monocrop 단일 경작을 하다
vast 광활한
genetically 유전적으로
uniform 동일한
boost 늘리다
yield 수확량; 생산하다; 굴복하다 (to)

04 Representing something graphically was a significant step beyond oral description of the objects and events being portrayed. (2016, 국회직 9급)

04
represent 나타내다, 표현하다
oral 구두의
portray 묘사하다

05 Maintaining and strengthening the relationship, rather than "winning" the argument, should always be your first priority. (2017, 법원직 9급)

05
argument 논쟁

06 Suspicious of the food he was being served at his boarding house, Dr. Georg de Hevesy, a Nobel Prize winner in chemistry in 1946, conducted a simple experiment at dinner one evening.

06
suspicious 의심하는
serve 제공하다
boarding house 하숙집
conduct 수행하다
experiment 실험

07 Simply asking people to estimate the length of time they are exposed to a train of stimuli shows that novel stimuli simply seem to last longer than repetitive or unremarkable ones. (2017, 지방직 9급)

07
estimate 추정하다
a train of 일련의
stimuli (stimulus의 복수) 자극
novel 새로운
repetitive 반복적인
unremarkable 눈에 띄지 않는

08 Asked to choose the two indicators that give them the best indication of how the economy is doing, only 32 percent of the public mentions news reports on government unemployment and cost of living statistics. (2016, 기상직 7급)

08
indicator 지표
indication 나타내는 것, 표시

② ……문장 맨 앞에 To RV가 나오면...

❖ 다음을 해석하세요.

01 To understand the true sequence of events by other clues is essential in reading a detective story.

01
sequence 연속
clue 단서
essential 필수적인
detective story 추리소설

02 To "win hands down" which means to "win easily" or "win with little or no effort" has its origins in horse racing. (2016, 법원직 9급)

02
win hands down 쉽게 이기다
horse racing 경마

03 To import new ideas from the West, Peter demanded that young Russians go abroad to study, and he invited Europeans to visit Russia. (2015, 기상직 7급)

03
import 수입하다

04 To entice the most experienced and skilled workers, the company developed a new pay scale for workers that has minimized profits and met all union demands. (2012, 서울시 9급)

04
entice 유도하다
scale 등급, 구조
minimize 최소화하다
union 조합

05 To have a good partnership with your doctor, it is important to talk about sensitive subjects, like marital or memory problems, even if you are embarrassed or uncomfortable. (2019, 법원직 9급)

05
sensitive 민감한
marital 결혼의, 부부의
embarrassed 부끄러운, 쑥스러운

06 To avoid the condition known as digital dementia, or forgetfulness, experts suggest remembering important phone numbers in your head, and concentrating when reading magazines or newspapers. (2014, 기상직 9급)

06
condition 증상
dementia 치매
forgetfulness 건망증
concentrate 집중하다

07 To address that problem of incentives and encourage more R&D investment, the government uses several policy tools, including appropriated spending for R&D activities, tax preferences for private sector research and development, and protection of intellectual property through the copyright and patent systems. (2014, 국가직 7급)

07
address 다루다
incentive 장려책
R&D 연구개발
appropriate 책정하다
preference 특혜; 선호
private 민간의
sector 부문
property 재산
copyright 저작권
patent 특허권

③ ······ 문장 중간에 RVing나 p.p.가 나오면...

❖ 다음을 해석하세요.

01 Astronomers today are convinced that people living thousands of years ago were studying the movement of the sky. (2011, 지방직 9급).

01
astronomer 천문학자
convince 확신시키다
thousands of 수천의

02 Children can benefit from learning how to use context clues and guessing the meaning from the context. (2016, 사회복지직 9급)

02
context 맥락, 문맥

03 In order to meet the demands of each course, Escoffier modernized meal preparation by dividing his kitchens into five different sections.
(2018, 법원직 9급)

03
demand 요구
modernize 현대화하다
preparation 준비

04 An infomercial is a television commercial lasting approximately thirty minutes and used to sell a product by convincing viewers that they must have the product. (2011, 국가직 9급)

04
infomercial 정보가 많은 광고
commercial 광고
approximately 거의

05 While the first step in alleviating poverty in the developing world is providing adequate food and shelter, long-term solution to the problem must focus on other issues. (2017, 경찰직 1차)

05
alleviate 완화시키다
poverty 빈곤
developing world 개발도상국
adequate 적절한
shelter 주거지

06 They devoted themselves to hours of unpaid work for the poor and helpless, never minding that few appreciated what they were doing for society.

06
devote oneself to ~에 전념하다
unpaid 무보수의
helpless 무력한
mind 언짢아하다, 상관하다
appreciate 감사하다

07 To become successful problem solvers, they have to appreciate the theory, recognizing the logical structure and reasoning behind the mathematical methods. (2010, 국가직 9급)

07
solver 해결사
appreciate 올바르게 인식하다
logical 논리적인
reasoning 추론

08 After several frightening minutes, they found a narrow ledge and climbed on to it, hoping the snow would stop and they could continue their descent. (2015, 법원직 9급)

08
frightening 끔찍한, 무서운
narrow 좁은
ledge 절벽에서 튀어나온 바위; 선반
descent 하강

09 Among Muslims in Egypt, the bereaved are encouraged to dwell at length on their grief, surrounded by others who relate to similarly tragic accounts and express their sorrow. (2022, 국가직 9급)

09
the bereaved 유족들
dwell on ~에 머무르다
relate to ~와 관련이 있다
account 이야기

10 To him, for instance, the mythical stories of gods fighting among themselves were allegories representing the forces of nature that oppose each other, such as fire and water. (2018, 법원직 9급)

10
mythical 신화상의
allegory 우화, 풍자
represent 대표하다, 대변하다
oppose 대항하다, 대립하다

11 The evidence so far collected by archeologists and paleontologists suggests that the cradle of humankind was in East Africa, about five million years ago, when the Australopithecines first appeared. (2011, 지방직 7급)

11
archeologist 고고학자
paleontologist 고생물학자
cradle 요람
humankind 인류, 인간
Australopithecine 오스트랄로피
테쿠스류(의)

12 Despite being the first person to actually build one, Joseph Dart claimed not to be the inventor of the elevator, saying instead that he had based his designs entirely on those of Oliver Evans. (2017, 지방직 7급)

12
claim 주장하다

13 Second, the telephone polls conducted tended to favor Dewey because in 1948, telephones were generally limited to wealthier households, and Dewey was mainly popular among elite voters. (2020, 경찰직 1차)

13
conduct 실시하다, 시행하다
favor 선호하다
voter 투표자, 유권자

14 Lamarck might explain that a kangaroo's powerful hind legs were the result of ancestors strengthening their legs by jumping and then passing that acquired leg strength on to the offspring. (2022, 국가직 9급)

14
hind 뒤쪽의
ancestor 조상
offspring. 자손, 새끼

15 Some heroes shine in the face of great adversity, performing amazing deeds in difficult situations; other heroes do their work quietly, unnoticed by most of us, but making a difference in the lives of other people.

15
adversity 역경
deed 행위
unnoticed 눈에 띄지 않는

16 The great explosion of scientific creativity in Europe was certainly helped by the sudden spread of information brought about by Gutenberg's use of movable type in printing and by the legitimation of everyday languages, which rapidly replaced Latin as the medium of discourse.

16
explosion 폭발
legitimation 합법화
medium 매개체
discourse 담론, 담화

④ ····· 문장 중간에 to RV가 나오면...

❖ 다음을 해석하세요.

01 The secret of life is not to do what one likes, but to try to like what one has to do. (2013, 국가직 9급)

01
secret 비결

02 The ancient Olympics provided athletes with an opportunity to prove their fitness and superiority, just like our modern games. (2018, 지방직 9급)

02
ancient 고대의
athlete (운동) 선수
fitness 건강
superiority 우월성
modern 현대의

03 The objective of some taxes on foreign imports is to protect an industry that produces goods vital to a nation's defense.

03
objective 목적
vital 필수적인
defense 방어

04 He believed that the nature of human beings is to be creative and that living a creative life is the key to human health and well-being.

(2017, 국가직 9급)

04
nature 본성
creative 창조적인

05 In one smile study, people were asked to hold a pencil lengthwise between their teeth to make themselves look like they are smiling.

(2015, 지방직 9급)

05
lengthwise 길게

06 Some writers argue that the best way to minimize the explosive quality of the present arms race is somehow to develop a stable balance of terror. (2014, 국가직 7급)

06
minimize 최소화하다
explosive 폭발적인
arms race 군비 확장 경쟁
somehow 어떻게든
stable 안정적인

07 Recent studies show that not self-control but pride, gratitude and compassion reduce the human mind's tendency to discount the value of the future, and help people succeed in life. (2018, 국회직 8급)

07
self-control 자제력
gratitude 감사
compassion 연민
discount 무시하다

08 Your culture maintains an implicit schedule for the right time to do many important things; for example, the right time to start dating, to finish college, to buy your own home, or to have a child. (2018, 경찰직 1차)

08
maintain 유지하다; 주장하다
implicit 암묵적인

<Further Study : be to 용법>

01 The meeting is to be held this afternoon. [예정]

02 You are to pay your debt as soon as possible. [의무]

03 Nothing was to be seen in the sky. [가능]

04 If you are to succeed, you must work hard. [의도]

05 He was never to come back to his country again. [운명]

06 Imagine that it's Saturday and you are to meet your friends at the mall at 12:00. [예정]

1. 시제

❶ 다음을 알맞은 시제의 형태로 고치고 그 의미를 생각하면서 해석하세요.

● 예제

현재 He studies English.

해석 그는 영어를 공부한다.

현재진행 He is studying English.

해석 그는 영어를 공부하고 있는 중이다.

과거 He studied English yesterday.

해석 그는 어제 영어를 공부했다.

과거진행 He was studying English when I saw him.

해석 내가 그를 봤을 때 그는 영어를 공부하고 있었다.

현재완료 He has studied English for 3 years.

해석 그는 3년간 영어를 공부해왔다.

과거완료 He had studied English for 3 years before he graduated from school.

해석 그는 학교를 졸업하기 전에 3년간 영어를 공부했었다.

미래완료 He will have studied English for 3 years when he graduates from school next year.

해석 그가 다음 해에 학교를 졸업할 때쯤에 그는 3년간 영어를 공부해 올 것이다.

---

01 현재 He <u>takes care of</u> his kids.

해석 그가 아이들을 <u>돌본다</u>.

현재진행 He _____ his kids.

해석 그가 아이들을 _____.

과거 He _____ his kids yesterday.

해석 그가 어제 아이들을 _____.

과거진행 He _____ his kids when I walked in the house.

해석 내가 집에 들어섰을 때, 그는 아이들을 _____.

현재완료 He _____ his kids for a week.

해석 그가 일주일 동안 아이들을 _____.

과거완료 He _____ his kids for a week.

해석 그가 일주일 동안 아이들을 _____.

미래완료 He _____ his kids for a week when I come back tomorrow.

해석 내가 내일 돌아올 때쯤에 그는 일주일 동안 아이들을 _____.

02 현재진행 It <u>is raining</u> now.

해석 지금 비가 <u>오고 있는 중이다</u>.

과거진행 It _____ when I came here.

해석 내가 여기 왔을 때 _____.

미래진행 It _____ when we go there tomorrow.

해석 내일 우리가 거기 갈 때 _____.

현재완료진행 It _____ for 5 hours.

해석 5시간째 _____.

과거완료진행 It _____ for 5 hours when I came here.

해석 내가 여기 왔을 때, 5시간째 _____.

미래완료진행 It _____ for 3 days when we come back tomorrow.

해석 내일 우리가 돌아올 때 3일째 _____.

Ⅱ 다음 두 문장의 의미 차이를 생각하며 해석하세요.

> ● 예제
>
> · The sun <u>rises</u> in the east. → 태양은 동쪽에서 <u>뜬다</u>.
> · Look! The sun <u>is rising</u> in the east. → 봐! 태양이 동쪽에서 <u>뜨고 있어</u>.

01 Nurses look after patients in hospitals.

→ 간호사는 병원에서 환자들을 _____.

The nurse is looking after patients in the hospital.

→ 그 간호사는 병원에서 환자들을 _____.

02 She has studied English for 3 hours.

→ 그녀는 3시간 동안 영어를 _____. (3시간 전부터 지금까지)

She studied English for 3 hours.

→ 그녀는 3시간 동안 영어를 _____. (과거에 3시간 정도를)

03 I will read this book three times if you buy it for me.

→ 만약 네가 이 책을 내게 사준다면 난 이 책을 세 번 _____.

I will have read this book three times if I read it again.

→ 내가 이 책을 한 번 더 읽는다면 난 이 책을 세 번 _____.

2. 능동/수동

❖ 다음 주어진 문장을 수동태 혹은 능동태로 바꾸세요.

● 예제

I <u>painted</u> this wall.

➡ <u>This wall <u>was painted</u> by me.</u>

[해석] 나는 이 벽을 칠했다. / 이 벽은 나에 의해 칠해졌다.

---

01 My sister <u>takes care of</u> him.

➡

[해석]

02 He <u>has painted</u> these pictures.

➡

[해석]

03 The light <u>was turned on</u> by them.

➡

[해석]

04 She <u>finished</u> her report yesterday.

➡

[해석]

05 They <u>are constructing</u> the building.

➡ _____

해석 _____

06 The problems <u>had been solved</u> by him.

➡ _____

해석 _____

07 She <u>had often seen</u> such a sight before.

➡ _____

해석 _____

08 Susan <u>has been writing</u> another novel this year.

➡ _____

해석 _____

09 This building <u>has been being reconstructed</u> for two years by them.

➡ _____

해석 _____

10 The police <u>asked</u> the suspect a lot of questions about the accident.

➡ _____

해석 _____

1. 가정법

❖ 다음 문장에서 가정법의 시제를 나타내는 표현에 밑줄을 긋고 시제를 쓴 후, 시제에 주의하면서 해석하세요.

> ● 예제
>
> If he <u>were</u> living, he <u>would be</u> twenty years old now.
>
> 시제 가정법 과거(현재 사실의 반대)
>
> 해석 만약 그가 살아 있다면, 이제 20살일 텐데.

01 I would see her every day if she lived here.

시제

해석

02 If it should rain tomorrow, I would cancel my trip.

시제

해석

03 If he had been honest, I would have employed him.

시제

해석

04 Had you asked me, I would have told you the answer.

시제 _____

해석 _____

05 Should their efforts succeed, a major ecological problem would be solved.

시제 _____

해석 _____

06 If it had not rained last night, the road would not be so muddy this morning.

시제 _____

해석 _____

07 If he had had a better knowledge of the mountain, he would not have died like that.

시제 _____

해석 _____

08 If Shakespeare were to return to life today, he would be amazed to find his plays being studied in schools.

시제 _____

해석 _____

2. 조동사

❖ 조동사의 의미를 생각하며 해석하세요.

● 예제

He **can** <u>speak</u> English well.

해석 그는 영어를 잘 말할 수 있다.

---

01 He **must** be an American.

해석 그는 미국인임이 _____.

02 She **may** have been drowned.

해석 그녀는 _____.

03 You **must** do the work at once.

해석 당신은 그 일을 즉시 _____.

04 She **can**not <u>stand</u> it any more.

해석 그녀는 더 이상 그것을 _____.

05 Sam **can**not have been hungry.

해석 Sam이 _____.

06 You **may** <u>go</u> there at any moment.

해석 당신은 언제라도 거기에 _____.

07 **Can** I <u>use</u> your pen for a moment?

해석 잠시만 당신의 펜을 _____?

08 Children **should** <u>listen to</u> their parents.

해석 아이들은 당연히 부모님 말씀을 _____.

09 You**'d have heeded** his warning.

해석   너는 그의 경고를 _____.

10 She **need** not have come here tonight.

해석   그녀는 오늘밤 여기 _____.

11 We **must** not play balls on big streets.

해석   우리는 큰길에서 공을 _____.

12 This book **may** be very interesting for you.

해석   이 책은 아마 당신에게 _____.

13 The virus **may** not have existed there before.

해석   그 바이러스는 이전에는 거기에 _____.

14 You **should** not play computer games too long.

해석   너는 당연히 컴퓨터 게임을 너무 오래 _____.

15 The plane **should** be landing right on schedule.

해석   그 비행기는 당연히 예정에 맞게 _____.

16 You **must** not have done it not to be punished.

해석   너는 벌을 받지 않으려고 그것을 _____.

17 Listening to music **may** not be helpful when you study.

해석   음악을 듣는 것은 공부할 때엔 _____.

3. 동사편 총정리

❖ 다음을 해석하세요.

01 Today many Native Americans are fighting their problems.

02 This issue had not been established legally in the United States.

(2010, 국가직 9급)

02
establish 규명하다
legally 합법적으로

03 As a last resort, you may have to accept their point of view. (2008, 국가직 7급)

03
resort 수단, 방책
point of view 관점

04 You cannot have felt the earthquake, for it was so slight.

04
slight 작은, 경미한

05 Lately, however, bats have become more popular because they eat mosquitoes. (2008, 국가직 7급)

05
lately 최근에
mosquito 모기

06 And afterwards I was very glad that the coolie had been killed by the elephant. (2008, 국가직 7급)

06
afterwards 나중에, 그 후
coolie 쿨리(인도·중국의 하층 노동자)

07 You might first want to read something about how the engine operates.

07
operate 작동하다

08 On the other hand, the water for the fields is taken from a number of small ponds or streams.

08
pond 연못
stream 시내

09 The sales clerk must have forgotten to remove the security tag when you purchased the choker. (2009, 국가직 7급)

09
sales clerk 판매원
security 보안
tag 꼬리표
choker 목에 꼭 끼는 목걸이

10 Over the years various systems of grading coins have been developed by antique coin specialists.

10
grade 등급을 매기다
antique 고대의
specialist 전문가

11 The cities themselves cannot be developed without the prior development of the rural areas.

11
prior 우선하는
rural 시골의

12 Sound waves can be generated electronically by synthesizing the different components of the sound waves. (2008, 지방직 9급)

12
sound wave 음파
generate 발생시키다
electronically 전자적으로
synthesize 합성하다
component 요소

13 Even though note-writing may take longer, some pretty busy people do it, including George Bush.

13
pretty 상당히, 꽤

14 Had the computer parts been delivered earlier, we could have been able to complete the project on time. (2009, 국가직 7급)

14
on time 제시간에

15 We should acknowledge that the environment we live in has been being updated ever since the dawn of civilization.

15
acknowledge 인정하다
update 갱신하다
dawn 새벽, 여명
civilization 문명

16 During her lifetime, she may really have felt like a nobody, for few people knew her outside of her small hometown.

16
nobody 쓸모없는 사람

17 The radio, the movie, and the airplane should have taught us that technology may be beneficent but may also serve evil purpose.

17
beneficent 이익이 되는

18 The difficulty could have been overcome — or might never have arisen — if the people involved had just treated one another with common courtesy. (2008, 지방직 9급)

18
overcome 극복하다
arise 발생하다
courtesy 예절

19 A number of tests have been being given to the quantitative analysis to make its result clear.

19
quantitative 양적인
analysis 분석

20 Although the Europeans may have practiced slavery on the largest scale, they were by no means the only people to bring slaves into their communities. (2021, 국가직 9급)

20
slavery 노예 제도
by no means 결코 ~이 아닌

그 밖의 핵심 구문 해석법

UNIT 1. It + be + 형/명 + to 부정사/that절

❖ 다음을 해석하세요.

01 It is an axiom of economics that as prices rise, consumers become more discriminating. (2021, 국가직 9급)

01
axiom 자명한 이치
discriminating 식별력[분별력]이 있는

02 There are many instances in our society in which it is entirely appropriate for people to play a power role over others. (2015, 지방직 9급)

02
instance 경우
entirely 전적으로
appropriate 적절한
power 권력

03 It is certainly important for children to learn to succeed; but it is just as important for them to learn not to fear failure. (2015, 지방직 9급)

03
certainly 분명히
fear 두려워하다

04 It is well known that vitamin D deficiency can affect one's muscles, bones and immunity and is even associated with cancer. (2015, 지방직 9급)

04
deficiency 결핍
affect 영향을 주다
immunity 면역력
be associated with ~와 관련되다
cancer 암

05 It is possible that chroniclers were encouraged by their Mongol employers to exaggerate the tales of cruelty so that the Mongols appeared more frightening to their enemies. (2016, 서울시 9급)

06 In Britain and some other European countries, it was the custom for women to have the right to propose marriage to the men of their choice.

07 It is important to remember that even when one group of speakers becomes totally isolated from other speakers, its language continues evolving. (2008, 지방직 7급)

08 No wonder it was said that the trial would affect the governor's race, because it set a supporter of capital punishment against an opponent. (2016, 경찰직 2차)

09 The most elusive element of all appears to be francium, which is so scarce that it is thought that our entire planet may contain, at any given moment, fewer than twenty francium atoms. (2014, 지방직 9급)

* S + V + it + 형용사[명사] + to부정사[that절]

01 In some cultures, people think it wrong to share their feelings and worries with others. (2014, 경찰직 2차)

02 Experiments make it clear that the analytical procedure adopted in the paper fully satisfies the requirements for further research.

* It ~ that 강조구문

01 It is his illness that makes him violent and dangerous.

02 It is in the second part of the book that the hero overcomes his drawback and learns a lesson.

UNIT 2. and/or의 용법

❖ 다음을 해석하세요.

01 Rituals like looking at your watch, reaching for a car key, and untying shoes are seldom forgotten. (2011, 국회직 8급)

01
ritual 의식
untie 풀다

02 Campus buses will leave the main hall every half an hour and make all of the regular stops along their routes around the campus. (2014, 국가직 9급)

02
regular 정기적인
stop 정차
route 경로

03 Getting a good night's sleep before the test and eating a nutritious breakfast will enhance your alertness and help you feel relaxed.

03
nutritious 영양분이 많은, 영양가가 높은
enhance 향상시키다
alertness 민첩함

04 The balls were first made of grass or leaves held together by strings, and later of pieces of animal skin sewn together and stuffed with feathers or hay.

04
string 끈, 줄
sew 꿰매다
stuff 채워 넣다
hay 건초

05 It's easy to lose objectivity or to overlook errors, inconsistencies, or problems when you have focused too intensely or for too long on a particular task. (2015, 법원직 9급)

05
objectivity 객관성
inconsistency 모순
intensely 강하게, 열심히

06 A device that accomplishes tasks similar to those a human can perform and that reacts to at least some changes in the environment is called a robot. (2011, 국회직 8급)

06
device 장치
accomplish 성취하다

07 Sports physicians recommend icing the bruised area, gently stretching and massaging the foot, and taking anti-inflammatory drugs to help alleviate the pain. (2020, 경찰직 1차)

07
bruised 멍든
anti-inflammatory 소염제(의)
alleviate 완화하다

08 The speed and extent of this dispersal have been largely controlled by humanity's ability to exploit the advantages and overcome the disadvantages presented by climate. (2011, 지방직 7급)

08
extent 범위
dispersal 확산
exploit 이용하다
overcome 극복하다
disadvantage 약점
present 주다, 제공하다

09 A suitable insurance policy should provide coverage for medical expenses arising from illness or accident prior to or during their vacation, loss of vacation money, and cancellation of the holiday.

09
suitable 적합한
insurance policy 보험 증권
coverage 보상 범위
cancellation 취소

10 The ant's abdomen ruptures, releasing a sticky yellow substance that will be lethal for both the defender and the attacker, permanently sticking them together and preventing the attacker from reaching the nest. (2016, 서울시 9급)

10
abdomen 복부
rupture 파열되다
release 방출하다
sticky 끈적끈적한
substance 물질
lethal 치명적인
defender 방어자
permanently 영원히

11 'Globalization' boosted trade, encouraged productivity gains and lowered prices, but critics alleged that it exploited the low-paid, was indifferent to environmental concerns and subjected the Third World to a monopolistic form of capitalism. (2021, 국가직 9급)

11
gain 개선, 향상
critic 비판하는 사람
allege 주장하다
exploit 착취하다
indifferent 무관심한
subject 종속시키다
monopolistic 독점적인

12 Adrenaline travels all over the body doing things such as widening the eyes to be on the lookout for signs of danger, pumping the heart faster to keep blood and extra hormones flowing, and tensing the skeletal muscles so they are ready to lash out at or run from the threat. (2020, 국가직 9급)

12
be on the lookout for ~을 지켜
보다, 경계하다
tense 긴장시키다
lash out at ~을 후려갈기다, 공격
하다

UNIT 3. 비교급·원급 해석법

❖ 다음을 해석하세요.

01 Parental guidance is no less important than school education.

(2016, 지방직 7급)

01
parental 부모의
guidance 지도

02 Few living things are linked together as intimately as bees and flowers. (2013, 국가직 9급)

02
intimately 친밀하게

03 The more we try to anticipate these problems, the better we can control them. (2017, 국가직 9급)

03
anticipate 예측하다

04 The greater the down payment a person makes, the smaller the monthly payments will be.

04
down payment 착수금

05 The moon is almost a perfect sphere; its diameter differs by no more than 1% in any direction. (2016, 서울시 9급)

05
sphere 구
diameter 지름
direction 방향

06 The harder you work, the more likely you are to get good grades, and the brighter your future will be.

06
grade 성적, 등급

07 The faster an astronomical object spins, the more it becomes bulged at the equator and flattened at the poles. (2016, 서울시 9급)

07
astronomical 천문(학상)의
spin 회전하다
bulge 불룩하다
equator 적도
flatten 납작해지다
pole 극지방

08 The school converted its athletic facilities into a shelter that housed as many as 500 displaced storm victims.

08
convert 전환시키다, 바꾸다
shelter 피난처
house 수용하다
displace (살던 곳에서) 쫓아내다

09 The department should be as helpful as possible and ensure that the system is properly restored by a qualified person. (2018, 소방직 9급)

09
department 부서
ensure 보장하다
properly 제대로
restore 복구하다
qualified 자격이 있는

10 If there's anyone in this assembly, any dear friend of Caesar's, I say to him that my love for Caesar was no less than his. (2015, 법원직 9급)

10
assembly 모임

11 Men always believe they need a way to make themselves seem more successful and charming than they really are. (2017, 국가직 9급)

11
charming 매력적인, 멋진

12 So far as you are wholly concentrated on bringing about a certain result, clearly the quicker and easier it is brought about the better.

12
so far as ~하는 한
wholly 전적으로
concentrate 집중하다
bring about ~을 가져오다, ~을 야기하다

13 The control of communication apprehension lies in removing as many of the areas of uncertainty and unfamiliarity as possible. (2016, 교육행정직 9급)

13
apprehension 불안
uncertainty 불확실성
unfamiliarity 생소함

14 Fats provide the body's best means of storing energy, a far more efficient energy source than either carbohydrates or proteins. (2017, 경찰직 1차)

14
fat 지방
means 수단
efficient 효과적인
source 원천
carbohydrate 탄수화물
protein 단백질

15 In the dry, rugged desert a saguaro cactus can live for more than 200 years, grow to a height of 60 feet, and have as many as 50 arms. (2017, 국회직 8급)

15
rugged 험악한, 거친
cactus 선인장

16 An economy as big as the United States can afford to place reasonable bets in all areas where it looks as if technology can be pushed forward. (2018, 경찰직 2차)

16
afford ~할 여유가 있다
reasonable 합리적인
bet 내기
push forward 계속 나아가다

17 Although the color advertisements did produce more attention, they did not attract as many readers per dollar as the black and white advertisements. (2017. 국가직 9급)

17
attention 관심
attract 끌어들이다

18 Processing a TV message is much more like the all-at-once processing of the ear than the linear processing of the eye reading a printed page.

18
process 처리하다
linear 선의, 직선 모양의

19 Since the optic nerve contains roughly eighteen times as many neurons as the cochlear nerve, we assume it transmits at least that much more information. (2017. 국가직 9급)

19
optic nerve 시신경
contain 포함하다
roughly 대략
cochlear nerve 달팽이 신경
assume 가정하다
transmit 전달하다

20 Coral reefs support more species per unit area than any other marine environment, including about 4,000 species of fish, 800 species of hard corals and hundreds of other species. (2016. 법원직 9급)

20
species 종
marine 해양의

21 A person who feels bad with reasonable regularity will enjoy the occasional period of feeling good far more than somebody who feels good so often that he is bored by it.

21
regularity 규칙적임, 패턴
occasional 가끔의
bore 지루하게 하다

22 The more people there are in a conversation, the less well you know them, and the more status differences among them, the more a conversation is like public speaking or report-talk. (2015, 서울시 7급)

23 The basking shark becomes fertile at the age of four and a pregnancy lasts for about two years, resulting in not more than six "baby-sharks," each measuring about 1.5 meters in length. (2017, 경찰직 1차)

23
fertile 가임기의, 비옥한
pregnancy 임신
last 지속되다
result in ~을 낳다, 야기하다

24 As we'll see, people who devote immense amount of time to political news can actually be more misinformed and less reasonable than those of us who spend far less time following politics. (2016, 기상직 7급)

24
devote 쏟다, 기울이다, 바치다
immense 엄청난
reasonable 합리적인

25 Managers who want people to take a more team-based approach with their people, for example, will almost certainly get better results by taking a more team-based approach themselves rather than just by making a speech on teamwork.

25
approach 접근법, 처리 방법

UNIT 4. 도치·생략·삽입 구문 해석법

❖ 다음을 해석하세요.

01 No sooner had he finished one task than he was asked to do another one. (2017, 지방직 7급)

02 The new deal will make possible the smooth transition of the Korean economy.

02
deal 거래, 합의
smooth 부드러운, 순조로운
transition 이행, 과도

03 Not everybody, European intellectuals argued, should go to high school. (2013, 지방직 7급)

03
intellectual 지식인

04 The statement does not make clear to us who will be affected by the new policy.

04
statement 진술, 서술, 성명
affect ~에 영향을 미치다
policy 정책

05 Just as a tree is known by the fruits it bears, so a man by the company he keeps.

05
bear (꽃이나 열매를) 피우다[맺다]
company 친구
keep 사귀다

06 Not only are people spending money they don't have, they're using it to buy things they don't need. (2021, 국가직 9급)

07 Lisa, who I remember was good at math in high school, is now specializing in Spanish literature in college.

07
specialize in ~을 전공하다

08 At the top, as we have seen, was the *scalco*, or steward, who was in charge of not only the kitchen, but also the dining room. (2018, 지방직 9급)

08
steward 관리인
be in charge of ~을 책임지다
dining room 식당

09 So unique is it among the lemurs that it has proven extremely difficult to determine which other lemurs are its closest relatives. (2018, 경찰직 3차)

09
unique 독특한
lemur 여우원숭이
extremely 매우
determine 결정하다
relative 친척

10 The stronger the vibrations of the sound, the greater the pressure difference between the high and the low, and the louder the sound.

10
vibration 떨림, 진동

11 An innovation may be anything — from new religious beliefs to a technological change — that is internally generated by members of the society. (2016, 지방직 9급)

11
religious 종교적인
belief 신념, 믿음
generate 만들어내다

12 Although both deal with negotiation, a mediator needs to maintain neutrality and an advocate partiality in order to avoid crossing over into each other's role.

12
negotiation 협상
mediator 중재자
neutrality 중립성
advocate 옹호자
partiality 편파성
cross over into ~쪽으로 넘어가다

13 Thus, the youth may identify with the aged, one gender with the other, and a reader of a particular limited social background with members of a different class or a different period.

13
identify 확인하다, 동일시하다
particular 특정한, 특별한

14 Only in the early twentieth century were several laws passed that restricted both the number of people who could come to the United States and where they could come from. (2016, 국회직 9급)

14
restrict 제한하다

15 The male moths live longer than the females, the former averaging about four weeks and the latter half that time or a little more.

15
moth 나방
former 전자의
average 평균 ~이 되다
latter 후자의

16 Eating seasonally and locally is a great way to maintain a healthy diet, observes a veteran food consultant and Korea's first accredited vegetable sommelier. (2016, 국가직 7급)

16
observe 말하다; 관찰하다
accredited 공인된

UNIT 5. 그 밖의 기타 구문 해석법

❖ 다음을 해석하세요.

01 The package, having been wrong addressed, reached him late and damaged. (2015, 국가직 9급)

01
wrong 잘못
address 주소를 쓰다

02 Perhaps you could get a guarantor — someone to sign for the loan for you. (2017, 서울시 9급)

02
guarantor 보증인
loan 대출

03 However, he was not smart enough to manage his income, and he died a poor man.

03
manage 관리하다
income 수입, 소득

04 Archaeological finds come in many forms — as artifacts, food remains, houses, human skeletons, and so on. (2018, 교육행정직 9급)

04
archaeological 고고학의
artifact 인공 유물
skeleton 뼈대, 골격

05 Many people believe that all they have to do to relieve an acute migraine headache is to take pain-killing drugs.

05
relieve 완화시키다
acute 급성의; 격심한, 극심한
migraine headache 편두통

06 By understanding our health-related motivations, we gain insights into barriers that keep us from enjoying better health as we age.

(2014, 국회직 8급)

06
motivation 동기
insight 통찰력
barrier 장벽

07 With the cord coming out of the back of the computer mouse, Douglas said the device reminded him of the rodent mouse and the name stuck. (2014, 사회복지직 9급)

07
rodent 설치류
stick 받아들여지다, 인정받다

08 Children's book awards have proliferated in recent years; today, there are well over 100 different awards and prizes by a variety of organizations. (2017, 국가직 9급)

08
proliferate 급증하다
a variety of 다양한, 많은
organization 기관

09 Microbats, the small, insect-eating bats found in North America, have tiny eyes that don't look like they'd be good for navigating in the dark and spotting prey. (2019, 서울시 9급)

09
tiny 아주 작은
navigate 항해하다, 돌아다니다
spot 발견하다, 찾다

10 The digital revolution means that sooner or later students and adults are going to need an entirely new set of skills: how to get information, where to find it, and how to use it.

10
revolution 혁명
sooner or later 조만간
entirely 완전히

11 With face-to-face conversations crowded out by online interactions, there are fears that an entire generation of young people consumed by social media is struggling to listen, make eye contact or read body language. (2017, 기상직 9급)

11
face-to-face 마주보는, 직접적인
conversation 대화
crowd out 밀어내다
interaction 상호작용
generation 세대
struggle 힘들어하다

12 Online shopping means it is easy for customers to buy without thinking, while major brands offer such cheap clothes that they can be treated like disposable items — worn two or three times and then thrown away. (2021, 국가직 9급)

12
disposable 일회용의

부록 1. 외운 대로 해석이 안 되는 의외의 영단어

01   Who, if not the government, would **house** these treasures for future generations?

02   To oversimplify, basic ideas **bubble** out of universities and laboratories in which a group of researchers work together.

03   We often dismiss new ideas that could **further** our growth simply because they do not fit within the general framework of our preconceived notions and self-conceptions.

04   Madagascar alone **harbors** some 8,000 species of flowering plants.

05 The screenplay requires so much filling in by our imagination that we cannot really **approximate** the experience of a film by reading a screenplay, and reading a screenplay is worthwhile only if we have already seen the film.

06 But empathy has its dark side: too much understanding and sensitivity, too much seeing things from the other's perspective, can **cloud** judgment and paralyze choice.

07 After local nuns **nursed** him through a serious illness in the 1940s, the grateful Matisse devoted himself to every detail of the chapel.

08 When people started to **plant** stored seed stock deliberately, they also began protecting their plants.

09 Paul wanted to buy some souvenirs, and he **spotted** a carving that he liked.

10 Most people tend to **rate** themselves more favorably on positive qualities and less unfavorably on negative ones than they are likely to actually merit when compared with external standards.

11-1 There was nothing **addressed** to her. It was her sixteenth birthday today, but there wasn't even a birthday card from her father.

11-2 The research **addresses** the question of how global vegetation has responded to changes in rainfall, temperature, and cloud cover patterns. Such climate factors determine how vegetation grows.

12-1 Researchers asked college student volunteers to think through a fantasy version of an experience and then evaluated the fantasy's effect on the **subjects** and on how things unfolded in reality.

12-2 **Subjecting** your entire hard-fought draft **to** cold, objective scrutiny is one of the toughest activities to master, but it is absolutely necessary.

12-3 Tradition was not static, but constantly **subject to** minute variations appropriate to people and their circumstances.

13 Biologists who study whale behavior generally have to be content with hanging around in boats, waiting for their subjects to **surface**.

14 Synthetic adhesives could **yield** transformative applications in robotics, industry, medicine, sports and clothing.

15 Lord Hailsham, minister of science and an ardent supporter of the test ban, was chosen to **head** the team from the United Kingdom.

16 The music of the time **mirrored** the feeling of optimism in the country.

17 Through their lanterns, rescue workers were able to **peer** into the cave and confirm that Shaul and Goldin were still alive.

18 The police have expressed **grave** concern about the missing child's safety.

Staff

Writer	심우철
Director	김지훈
Researcher	노윤기 / 정규리 / 장은영
Design	강현구
Manufacture	김승훈
Marketing	윤대규 / 한은지 / 장승재

발행일   2022년 12월 30일 (개정 5판 2쇄)

내용문의 http://cafe.naver.com/shimson2000